Bee Incredible

The Dao of the Bee

Author: Sara Beaumont-Connop

Illustrator: Michael Beaumont-Connop

© Copyright Sara Beaumont-Connop

The right of Sara Beaumont-Connop to be identified as the author of this work has been asserted by her in accordance with the Copyright, Designs and Patents Act.

All rights reserved. No part of this publication may be reproduced, stored in, or introduced into a retrieval system, or transmitted in any form or by any means (electronic, mechanical, photocopying, recording, or otherwise) without the prior written permission of the publisher. Any person who does any unauthorized act in relation to this publication may be liable to criminal prosecution and civil claims for damages.

or cover other than This book is sold subject to the condition that it shall not, by way of trade or otherwise, be lent, re-sold, hired out, or otherwise circulated without the publisher's prior consent in any form of binding that in which it is published and without a similar condition, including this condition, being imposed on the subsequent purchaser.

Other titles from Sara Beaumont-Connop:

You are the Horse and You are the Rider 2018.

The Fire Within: An Antipodean Escape 2023.

The Monkey Magicians of the Son Tra Mountains 2024.

The Riddle of the Rainbird 2024.

A mighty Bodhi tree flourished all the way to the 15th cosmic cascade, serving as a sky stairway, far beyond the 16th empyrean universe, and into the celestial empire of The Immortals.

Therein dwelt a honeybee Queen of such dazzling loveliness, that her name was ever upon the tongues of minstrels, one whose heart was even more exquisite than her form.

She was an Apis, a honeybee, a primordial being, and as such, undeniably magnificent; for the sunlight, refracted and diffused in the winds, gave her translucent pearlescent-golden body, all the colour spectrum.

Her name: Song Li, a Queen majestic, vigorous and graceful of movement.

In shape, she resembled a cylindrical helix, in three dimensions, slightly twisted; and when at rest, to a slight spiral curve.

When traveling, she straightened out with quick, successive buzzes, each one sending her flying ahead a couple of elongated lengths.

One languorous Spring day, Song Li flew into the heavenly orchard, playing her Sao flute, humming in an argentine harmony, buzzing through the aureate apricot blossoms, of the celestial palace garden.

So long did she tarry in her melodic meditation, on that silvery stream, that she sadly forgot her solemn duty, to her swelling swarms, who anxiously awaited her in the primeval jungles, of the Son Tra mountains, a place, that from the eastern sea, emerged with towering crests.

These were marble corrugations, and Cretaceous rocks, precipitous cliffs, and prodigious pinnacles.

Atop the carmine promontories, iridescent sunbirds sang in pairs, and before the razor-sharp ridges, spindle horned Saola silently rested.

At the summit was heard the cry of golden fireback pheasants, and in and out of granitic sea-grottoes, the strides of blue crested hadrosaurs, with trails of diamonds down their throats, were seen.

In the dipterocarp forest were caramel brown, sika deer; Ben-bi, an immortal dragon turtle, and nine, snowy tailed foxes; on the trees were Chim lac birds, and crimson, statuesque, sarus cranes; unique grasses, and blossoms that never shrivelled. Jade pines, and chanteuse cypresses eternally kept their spring, and divine banyans were ever fig bearing; even the

towering bamboos often captured the clouds; this was the Earth's Eden, the great axis in ten thousand eons unaltered.

Finally, Song Li returned to the Empyrean sky temple, only to be summoned by Lieu Hanh, the mother goddess of nature, ruler of earthen dominions, Empress of the azure Empyrean realm, below the sixteenth celestial universe.

Her magnificent face, like a snow moon, a gaze like autumnal water, small cherry lips, and a tiny willowy waist. Her features were striking enough to drown fishes, and elevate wild birds, and her complexion would cause the lunar orb to hide and put apple blossoms to shame.

Supreme ruler, Empress Lieu Hanh, demanded that Song Li relinquish her crown, as Queen of the honeybees, for she had forgotten her loyalty to her esteemed subjects, her greatest responsibility, to continually restore harmony and balance, in the natural world order.

"As a flower that is lovely and beautiful, but is scentless- even so, fruitless is the well-spoken word, of one who practices it not."

As the Proverb says.

Goddess Lieu Hanh angrily commanded, that as a punishment for her terrible irresponsibly, Song Li, miserable bee, be dethroned, and banished from the upper realms, the marble mountain peaks, and that all her hives be discontinued.

In abject despair, Song Li tore her beautiful, ornate winged raiment, to shreds, and as Lieu Hanh waved her mystical scepter, the disgraced apian then fell down, through the mist woven clouds, on the tears of the sun. When she finally hit the hard stone of the earth, the amber rocks shattered, and then encapsulated her, in a hexagonal prism.

There she lay, entrapped elliptically for many millennia, however, it was said by the sages, that Song Li's heart was even more beauteous than her form, and that she had closed her eyes, and opened her central beeing, listening closely to her heart beats, and heard her hive calling:

"Oh, Queen, Song Li! What laxity of mind! Why did you stay away for such a long time, and leave us here, longing for your return, like someone hungering and thirsting?"

"How can I make amends for my transgressions?" Song Li cried out in her anguished guilt, from her amber chamber.

Lieu Hanh, merciful goddess of Gaia, (nu than Trai Dat), sent her most celebrated messengers to her servant, Song Li, with a scrolled decree:

"If a Queen lacks trustworthiness, it is difficult to know what she can attain", they announced in unison.

Song Li's whole beeing shriveled in shame, and she cried, "even if I have to wander with the clouds, to the corners of the ends of the oceans, or journey to the distant fringes of the earth, I intend to repair the catastrophe, that I have wrought upon my charges, the sacred bees," she vowed.

The mother goddess challenged the penitent: "Song Li, you must stare into the heart of the magnanimous mountain, and read the secret texts contained therein".

Song Li focused herself on the very core of that massif, and there she studied these sagacious words,

The mind that has conceived a plan of living

Must never lose sight of the Chaos

Against which, that pattern was conceived.

At last, Song Li realised, that even her exulted existence, was not eternal, all things changed and were renewed by nature itself.

Song Li cried at the impermanence of her kind, but she also realised, seeking eternity for only herself, was like 'trying to scoop the moon's reflection from water'.

In silent moments of open clarity, she thought of the universal wisdom; the Dao of the bees:

'Everything that lives, esteem's its own life.

If dependents are abandoned, they must be cared for.

Nature gives life, and takes it away, this is the principle of nature.

Now if a beeing of duty, forsakes its adherents and they die, this is not the way of the cosmos.

If this is seen happening, and nothing is done, then that individual does not have a compassionate heart.

Matriarchs come with a gift. In general, all creatures between earth and sky, have ancestry and animation, and are certain to be blessed with awareness, there are none, which do not cherish their kin.

Male and female procreate together, mother and infant keep close together, they avoid the open clearings, and seek shelter, avoid cold, and seek out warmth, live in broods, and sojourn in clusters.

The young are protected and nourished by the adult, they will lead each other to water and call out to each other when they find food.

But since the bees were banished from the mountains, because of Song Li's forgetfulness, one by one, the flowers, and the fruit of the peninsula, failed or disappeared.

One by one, the creatures who ate the fruits and the flowers starved, the trees fell, and devastation came to the surrounding lands.

Finally, after much suffering, the jade empress, Lieu Hanh, said to her courteous courtiers: "this beeing from the world below, is born of the essences of heaven and earth, and she needs our compassion".

So, the great ruler called out to the desolate bee, "are you ready for your destiny, as a supplicant?"

"For there are many challenges for you, Song Li, to surmount; with this great dynastic obligation, from great abundance comes great commitment."

Lieu Hanh proclaimed, "many are the turns of Queenship, and you have to firstly reincarnate into a virgin Queen bee and earn your place among a new hive!"

In a dream that precluded time, a metamorphosis was taking place for the bee who would be Queen.

Song Li floated, encapsulated in rich royal jelly, and all she could do was consume its rich, sugary goodness, into her beeing.

As she developed, from egg to larvae, from far away she heard a creative rhyme:

"Who can hear below the bottomless cliff,

Beneath the shadowless tree.

The nightingales call for the dawn of Spring?

And in a whispered moment she heard:

"If you want to really live,

Don't act obliviously of your destiny."

Finally, Song Li found herself stretched out, head down, casting off her entire outer body layer, to reveal a new one, over and over again, she shed her entire outer body, eye surfaces, and inner stomach linings.

For three full days, Song Li was as small as a grain of pearly rice, a glistening grub, being fed copious amounts of Gelee Royale.

After ten days of transformations, a thin, silk cord, emanated from spinners in Song Li's lower abdomen, by now, she felt nothing in the world was difficult, if she set her mind to it, so she made a magic sign, recited an incantation, clenched her two stomachs tightly, and shook her whole body; then she jumped right up, and somersaulted forward until she had completed 80 somersaults. Finally, a fine veil of silken, snow-white thread, surrounded the Queen's cell, and she fell into a somnolent sleeping state, unfurled and elongated, legs outstretched.

Four delicate, diaphanous wings grew each side of Song Li's transmuting body, pale and gossamer, but strong as the wind, they would carry her far.

Pastel pink were her compound, hexagonal eyes on either side of her head, morphing into lilac, then violet purple, and at last her vision was colour coordinated.

In a span of ten days, the rest of her transfiguration continued apace, Song Li's imago, a unique final Queen bee-design was complete!

Distantly, Song Li heard sounds of chewing, through the hard, bisque, top cap of wax that covered her cup-like cylinder, she felt ultimately released, emerging out, onto the rim of the satiny cocoon.

Nursery worker bees surrounded their creation, as she stood beautiful, and formidable as the sunrise, and the twilight, and the snow upon the mountains,

fearsome as the tempest and lightning! Stronger than the foundations of the earth. All that saw her, adored her, and rejoiced.

Here was first born, Queen Song Li, the secrecy of her existence fallen from her, her head, adorned with a crown of golden fuzz, and her bright visage, released from its bondage, her dark eyes, purple as sapphires, hard and fell, wary of rivals.

A needled sword was in her abdomen, and she raised her tarsus claws against any onslaught.

Song Li stood in the middle of her hexadic chamber, her smooth, sharpened stinger gleaming, and when she espied other royal maiden bees hatching about her, she made such a war cry, of piping and tooting, in that brooding space, that all who heard her shook with dread.

At once, battle was upon her, her opponents beat their whipping wings, and the wind was tumultuous, there could only Bee one Queen!

Again and again, they wrested into the air, swiftly coming down upon each other, striking with claw, and stinger.

Still, she did not quail; damsel of the heavenly temple, child of a nature goddess, slender, but as a steel stiletto, fair, but terrible.

A swift stoke she dealt, skilled and deadly. Song Li stung again, and again, her victims falling aside like pebbles.

Worker bees watched applauding, as their chosen Queen showed her qualities, and willingness, to fight to the death for the hive, her spirit glowed, like a dancing rainbow.

On a day that began with a sky full of devine aura, Empress Lieu Hanh called to Song Li, in her virgin hive, "Oh repentant disciple, a monstrous creature will challenge you, for the very existence of your exceptional honeybees.

He is a great beast, with a ebony, silver helmet, that glistens in the sunlight, and on his body, a dark, silken robe, which sways in the wind; ten spans, the width of his waist; thirty feet, the length of his frame; he blows from his throat, a venom most vile, and lethal.

His title: 'Vespa wasp of chaos,' larger by far than a honeybee, more fearsome of frame and form, his strong mandibles crush and dismember, whilst still masticating his apian prey. Always armoured against bee stings, he and his kind hunt bees, hawking unsuspecting insects from the moist, still atmosphere, until finally, they locate bee-nests to predicate their mass slaughter upon.

Beeware his darkened form, as it flies against the sun and puts out its light, for he is on his way as I speak." Cried Lieu Hanh.

Then, even whilst Queen Song Li, was holding court in the bejeweled assembly hall, in the hexadic palace of Golden Arches, Lieu Hanh, monarch of heaven and earth commanded her adherent to begin defending her hive.

Out swished a swirl of bedazzling bees, but not just any labouring apis, these were guard and solider bees, defense of the realm bees!

They looked like tiny pieces of confetti, thrown into the air, but before Song Li's very gaze, they changed into three thousand bee sentinels; they were so keen of sight, and swift of flight, they could not be wounded by sword or spear.

Their Queen marveled at them, skipping and jumping, they rushed out at the mountains, ready to take on anyone or anything. The bee Queen's heart leapt with joy, at the sight of these fearless, flying warriors, and she gave thanks for their creation.

After Song Li heeded the goddess's warning, about the gruesome brute, she knew it was time her squad to practice war!

Calling to her charges, she commanded them: "Victory and defeat are the common experiences of a solider, but we 'all live and die' by your defense," she declared.

She looked out at her minions, and there she saw a swarm of apis, neatly positioned in an array, resembling a coiled dragon. They, who had set their whole beings on defending the hive!

Bowing in front of their illustrious leader, all the guard bees lined up, in their hexagonal squadrons.

They all began to sharpen their stingers, and when they finished, the drove went on a scouting mission, to find safe, secure, cavity sites to defend, placing guard patrols, and arranging sentry duties, against the invader. They gathered buffalo dung, as proof against the predator, and they placed it around the hive entrance.

They rehearsed, drilled, and synchronised their body shaking shimmer, to warn and repel their enemies, throughout the frigid sloughing breeze, and the murky dreadful fog.

On the surface of the colony, the colourful banners of the guard bees fluttered; and their lancet stingers, glimmered in the sunlight.

There were row upon row of opposition eyes, watching intently, and coat upon coat of saffron, yellow, chitinous exoskeletons, row upon row of translucent wings, beating, blasting, and buzzing, echoed in the skies.

Suddenly, the Vespa wasp's shadow darkened the nest door, Song Li opened her abdomen, releasing reeling waves of ambrosial fragrance, that sent the defenders into a state of stable solidarity. Special Queen bee pheromones diffused about them, stimulating the 'stay together, be strong' messages in their nervous systems.

Then hundreds upon hundreds of sentry bees, spread out over the hive entry, and began in unison to thrust up their metasoma abdomens, up in the air at angle of ninety degrees.

Menacingly, the horrid hornet, swooped down closer, and closer to the shaking, shimmering wave of honeybees, and as he approached, all he could see was a sea of sparkling ripples, waving in constant motion.

Visually, it began to confuse and irritate the great, black beast. The bee's undulating tsunami agitated the villainous vespa, who veered off the course of his evil intent; the inside of the hive, into the shadows of crowded trees in the dense juniper forest he careened, finally, blindly, crashing into one of them!

The soldier bee's frisson, lasted till the air was rid of birds fluttering by, and all flying insects were returned to their homes.

The whole world was becalmed by the disturbance, bedimmed, by the razzle-dazzle of the bees aerobic, shimmering, rumpus.

The clamour and glittering disturbed even the inhabitants of the paradise at the Devine temple, but Empress, Lieu Hanh, sat at serene ease, on her throne of solid silver, satisfied her words were now personified in deeds.

Queen bee, Song Li, looked upon her apian warriors, and was gratified.

On another, auspicious springtime day, from the Imperial tower of transfiguration, tranquil sovereign, Leiu Hanh called:

"Now you have had your coronation, Song Li, favourable bee Queen, accepted by the hive-mind of your esteemed workers,

I will gift to you 5 talismans.

Your instinctual intelligence has the ability to serve as the ground for all worldly experiences.

With the first, tourmaline-green talisman's endowment, the quality of Earth, existing in body and in mind, you will have two stomachs, one for eating, and one for storing nectar, and processing it into honey, and five eyes, to see all around your environs, two compound eyes on the sides of your face, for seeing shapes, and three small eyes on your crown, to see ultraviolet light spectrums.

The second, sapphire-blue talisman, water: is that of continuity, and adaptability, you and your progeny shall bee able to taste with your feet, especially attuned to salts, found in water sources, that your scouts seek out.

You will bee able to use water, collected in the pollen baskets on your hind legs, to tone down heated moments in your hive.

Third, ruby-red talisman, fire, the clarity to perceive, bees will have a sense of smell, that is fifty times more powerful than a dog's, this will protect you from many dangers you will encounter, including smoke.

When fire threatens the forgotten forest, you will detect it first, and leave the hive for safer climes.

Fourth, pearl-white talisman, Air, for continuous movement. Bees will be able to flap your wings, 230 times per second, your wings will move up and down, and also rotate, for aerodynamic performance.

Many escapes from peril can bee made with speed.

When you wave your antennae in the air, more than 300 taste receptors will bee engaged.

And the last, topaz-yellow talisman I bestow, is Space, for its unlimited emptiness, this boon is only for you, Song Li resident Queen, only royalty can lay the 2,000 eggs per day, 200,000 eggs per year, in the empty cups of hexagonal cells, only she can create the hives future from space.

As each of nature's tribulations confront you and your hive, remember, nothing in the world is difficult, only the mind makes it so, make a magic sign, recite the incantation, clench your stomachs tightly, shake your body, and spray elixir onto the wax hexagon floors, and your bees will perceive your messages".

So commanded, great goddess of Gaia, Lieu Hanh.

Celestial messengers sang out the verse of the philosophers:

'Great was the creative principle,

Supreme the female,

They make all things,

In obedience with divine nature'

It was now late spring. Song Li knew she had to visit the great, drone congregation area, and find drone mates, worthy of fathering her auspicious offspring.

But she would not be easily caught, her favourite amusement would be this race. "Whom so ever is so swift that he can catch me, will win the prize of my courtship."

Meanwhile, far away, dwelt a fire-phoenix mountain born bee, drone Tran Vien, strong in courage and mind.

He left the mount and flew to catch a fair wind. This particular male bee was sharp sighted, with eyes that covered most of his head, and his large, snowy wings, were broader than his female cousins, and his abdomen, stouter.

On this inquisitive drone's back, was a curious pattern of ink black triangles, laid tip to tip, like an hourglass, drawn on a glossy, golden background.

He drifted across verdant mountains sides, to seek the glorious prize.

Determined in heart and mind, to achieve remarkable things, to bee ahead of the drone comet.

Tran Vien was not handsome, in bee conventional ways, and his wide, flight wings, were a bit smaller than his peers, but he could outmaneuver his drone competitors, if not out fly them with speed.

Yet, he knew he was cunning, and he felt he was brave, and he wanted to win the red thread of courtship, that made Song Li, Queen bee, his bride for all to see.

He pondered much on his dilemma, as the great, drone race for the Queen, was only days away.

He buzzed, meditatively, around the trunk of a great banyan tree, thinking and thinking, how could he successfully catch the Queen in her messianic flight?

When all at once, a wizened drone elder, glided out of its glistening, chanteuse green branches.

He bowed to the young seeker, and said:

"If you want to catch the exquisite Queen, Song Li, you must soar to the lake of the slanting sun, and three moons, there, you must ask great grandfather, jade turtle, for his favour, only he has Emperor Longs esteem.

Venerable jade turtle, Ben-bi, his soft shell, a formidable fortress of longevity, adorned with intricate divine patterns, tasked honourable drone Tran Vien, to ask all of the creatures of the mountainside, to stop bringing offerings, to the Hoan Kiel lake, as these were polluting the clean, clear, crystalline waters, in which he swam, and they drank.

"Your final quest is to find a me a companion, to accompany me to live in my pagoda tower, at the centre of the illustrious Jasper Lake, explained Ben-bi. "For these favours I would gift you, Tran Vien, with two, enchanted, roseate apricots, from the celestial temple gardens, with their ambrosial fragrance, and spherical shape.

These beewitching fruits, were grown and tended, by the imperial mother of the emerald pool herself, those that ripened first, glowed like faces, reddened with fire, but now, sunbeams reveal their cinnabar charms.

When Queen Song Li sees these first fruits thrown before her, she will be momentarily distracted, giving you, your chance for immortality, go well, faithful Tran Vien," called the venerated one, Ben-bi, masterful turtle of cloudless waters.

In a sky full of the purest, crystalline mists, with sparkling light, and rainbow clouds passing ceaselessly, where the cries of white cranes pierced the heavens, Tran Vien wove his way, around every beast, bird, and insect, to tell them of the ancient spiritual turtle in his lake, with the turtle tower.

All were humbled, by learning of the plight of the most sacred sage, and his beautiful lake, with all the offerings debris poisoning the waters.

They began to realise that the marvelous jasper lake, was a mystical mirror, a reflection of the harmony, balance, and health of the lake, mountains, and inhabitants too.

Tran Vien searched diligently for a consort, for the stately old terrapin, it seemed to him, he had no chance of meeting anyone.

He thought there would certainly be someone living beyond the northern lake shore, as he had already visited the western, southern and eastern, with no success.

There, in the land of flaming flowers, on the highest peak, Fanispan; Tran Vien, finally espied a long, mysterious creature, writhing amongst a sphere of gleaming, glowing, amber flames, darting its blunt nose along the ground, and twisting the eighteen feet of its body, agonizingly around about.

Biting the long, scaly tail, the iridescent individual, wheeled itself into an eternal circle, and cried out, "I am a king cobra, who has been punished for not controlling my anger, and striking the buffalo of the Lord of the imperial monastery.

My punishment is to be captured in this unfortunate inferno, whilst trying to shed my skin, now I can never renew myself, by letting go of angry emotions, and the past problems. If are willing to release me, I will reward you in any way I can," the cobra moaned deliriously.

"Are you willing to follow me to the Lake, and meet with the revered elder, Turtle Ben-bi," enquired the intrepid Tran Vien.

"Anything, I will try any remedy, to this awful perdition, if you will but release me from my torment," wept the sobbing serpent.

Tran Vien sprinkled a few drops of magical water, that he had been gifted from grandfather turtle's lake. He began to fan his wings, and it began to blow, and blow, and blow the blazing fires engulfing the Cobra out.

Still, the wriggling snake lay captivated by its coils, encapsulated in dead, old, scaley skin, and Tran Vien thought hard on how to release the snake's dilemma.

Finally, he recollected the waggle dance of the bees, with infinity, woven into the rhythmic movements, he began to weave and dip around the basilisk, guiding it to crawl, and flip, as it was shedding its final incarnation of skin.

Tran Vien promenaded down a centre line, then waltzed, in circular patterns, clockwise, and anticlockwise, as if he were indicating where a nectar feast could be found, making a central bee-line, to show the direction from the sun and the journey home, each movement representing the S transformation, beginning with weak to healthy.

At last, the cobra felt reprieved, and then rose up from the depths of despair, with renewed vitality, letting go of his layers of past grief, anger, and love lost.

Belatedly, the king cobra had returned to its natural karmic state of wood and learnt how to manage its negative emotions with studied, patient, lithesome movements.

Ben-bi was overjoyed to welcome the contrite cobra, into the turtle tower pagoda, and Tran Vien left the spiritual master, armed with the enchanted apricots to gain his advantage.

Time went by delicately, and it was again early Spring. Tran Vien could see sage green gilding on the mountain woodland, and viridian sprouts of grass appearing. Apple blossoms were all fallen, and the banyan leaves softly budding.

In an open clearing, surrounded by ancient, verdant Ficus trees, the drone congregation was buzzing with excitement, for it was rumoured, that exulted Queen Song Li, would be flying her one and only, nuptial flight, on this very tranquil, serene, Spring afternoon; and whomsoever won the race to catch her, would bee her life-mate, and the foundation of all of her egg offspring forever!

All the drone suitors milled about in a wide arc, forming a huge cone, thousands of male bees, and only one opportunity.

How long, how short -

Drones have their span of ninety days,

He lives, he mates, he dies

Each preordained by fate.

Flying high, one hundred feet above the ground, Tran Vien meditated on the wisdom of Ben-bi's words:

"He who knows how to prevail, will not prolong his contest!

He who is a virtuoso of positions, will not engage in direct combat!

He who knows how to struggle, will not suffer defeat!

And He who knows how to lose, will not fear!"

Before the hall of the bee brood, Song Li set her flight wings and released the incense of her pheromones into the azure atmosphere. A swarm of drones recognised their prize transforming itself, into myriad shafts of flaming light, a comet chasing the sun!

Tran Vien flew as fast as he could and threw down the first aureate apricot. Song Li saw the sparkling sphere, and blinked in its tender lustre, veering slightly to the right.

"The truth of nirvana can never be realised without faith and perseverance," Tran Viet thought, when his wing muscles began to ache, and spasm.

Suffering his fate, he kept true to his course, faltering for a second only, as he called on his nature to prove efficacious.

Then, just as a whirling strand of bright spangled drones levelled with him, Tran Vien threw out his last fruit, the Queen bee again diverged, this time to the left, just long enough for Tran Vien to see her, catch up, and plant his victorious seed in her body, completing his quest for eternity!

His body fell to the ground, lifeless, his spirit released, no longer that of an ordinary drone. Tran Vien, strong and heroic, ascended to higher realms, he flew where the stars shine on the pearl lotus, and in the shades of jade willows where the parrots speak, and the peacock's call.

Countless shafts of hallowed luminescence found their way into the great promise hive, as hexangular waxen shapes took form, under the auspices, of the maiden wax producing bee's directions.

Each chamber carefully shaped by these magical bee's mandibles, formed into protective scales for larvae, and pupal protection and honey containment.

Song Li knew her very existence depended on her creative performance; her busy bees were watching her every move. With the speed of light, she placed thousands and thousands of tiny, pearlescent eggs, in every one of the six-sided cell cases; while outside, a favourable wind blew gently, and the omnific sun, shone brightly.

And Song Li's golden promise hive prospered, in the springtime, they gathered lotus, and rosemary flowers for nectar and pollen. In summer, they went in search of yellow mai, and lavenders, to make heavenly honey. In the autumn, they amassed sunflowers and goldenrod blooms, to ward off lean times. In the late winter, they searched for snowdrops and witch hazel, to live out the year.

The celestial scribes wrote: 'Honey represents the reciprocity at the heart of things, all must share its worth, this understanding, is the source of wisdom on Earth.

When baby Cinder-bee hatched, she was just a mite smaller than her siblings. And due to her smaller size, she was not a happy little worker bee, for she was just a simple maid.

Cinderbee wanted to bee special, she did not favour the flavour of cocoon eating, the wax was not to her sweet taste, the endless hive cleaning, so the older nurse bees could reuse the brood cells for more new eggs, was boring.

Then, the worst curse of all, the thing for which she had no stomach, even with two in lieu, was to face death itself, in her first few days of life. When, with the demise of bees who died, it was she, who had to take them from the hive, they were to be disposed of, these, who were no longer alive.

Smallest Cinder-bee shuddered at all this tragedy, and she was afraid.

Her older, wiser, sisters, severely chastised the fanciful child, for beeing spoilt and totally wild: "she would see when she was older, what happens to freeloaders."

Nursery worker bees, kept the nest temperature always a constant 34 -36

Celsius for the brood area, where the new babies were hatched and raised.

If the chamber was too hot, the nurses would fan the heated atmosphere with their mellifluously, efficient wings.

One day, Cinderbee was lazily cleaning in a darker arena of the beehive, she was thinking the most alarming thoughts, of running away.

Suddenly, she felt stalked by a terrible beast she did not know, but its drum beats upon her chest, told her something of its malignancy, she smelt a terrible stench, a foul reek it was, and alas, the small bee did nothing but panic, for she had not listened to the wisdom of her elders.

She had thought that from sun, and moon, and star, they were safe in their blessed home of the golden promise hive, but now a cold, silver, slither of moonlight had descended, right into the very heart of the hive!

Cinderbee looked before her, she saw a greyness, which the radiance of the golden promise hive did not illuminate, as if it were shadow, that no light could dissipate. Trembling, she looked up, in time to see a long, dark figure, like a phantom, alongside the smooth, waxen, wall crevices.

The small bee shrank back in horror, an ashy, brown Greater wax moth, she had only heard buzzing rumours about these, when the older worker bees droned of nightmares.

"What could she do, oh what could she, a very minuscule bee do?" She hummed anxiously.

In terrified turmoil, Cinderbee turned to escape, but as she was rushing for a way out, she caught a glimpse of herself in a shiny, wax, wall mirror, in it she saw her beauteous uniform, of black and gold bands, her wondrous, waving antennae, with 300 taste buds, and her marvelous quintet eyes.

Cinderbee realised that she was special, in the same way as every other worker bee in the nest, she belonged in this mysterious, magical realm, with everybody else, they were her sisters, her brothers, they all had kinship with her majestic mother, Queen Song Li, and she was theirs.

She had just been afraid of fitting in, now she understood, this marvelous apiarian family was her reason for bee-ing, they made her life worthwhile, and at this very moment they needed her, especially now, a great threat had invaded their lives.

Cinderbee flittered her wispy, white wings, and flew like the wind to her older siblings, to raise the alarm

Every artisan bee in the hive went on high alert, racing to battle stations, they all knew the ghastly jeopardy, their hive was braving.

For the greater wax moth, left its eggs in the hive wall crevices, and when the moth worms hatched, they burrowed through the honeycombs, feeding on the wax, killing the bee larvae, and ruining the honey storage cells!

Soldier-bees zoomed in to cool the hive down, with icy water from frigid mountain streams.

The bees fanned this chilled liquid from their backs, into the infected brood areas to bring the temperature down to minus 7.

Sticky propolis, made from a resinous substance obtained from plants, was distributed like glue, to gum up the crevices and cracks, preventing their deadly nemesis from gaining access.

The malignant moth had left behind a trail of webbing and faeces, and

Cinderbee, with other bee-labourers, gathered their cleaning material, collecting detritus, and expelling the last remnants of the evil infiltrator.

At last, the golden promise hive was once again restored to its former glory, order and peace reigned.

But what of tiny Cinderbee? What was her reality?

Queen Song Li was very pleased with her recalcitrant mini bee, she made Cinderbee, a maiden of her royal chamber, and only Cinderbee groomed her long, lustrous antennae, and fed her royal jelly, carefully.

In the dead of night, Queen Song Li lay in a dream, without light. Then she saw the young moon rising, and under its thin light, there loomed a black wall of rock, pierced by a dark arch, like a great gate.

It seemed to Song Li that she was lifted up, and passing over she saw the majestic, celestial temple, bathed in sinister obscurity, and on its top rested a devilish figure.

A large, black, dragon mantis from the evil depths, flew into Lieu Hanh's palace, and blew his hot, blasting breath, all over the beautiful building.

All of the little, ornamental dragons, on the high, titled eaves, of the green roofs, sparked scarlet, shivering to the tips of their gilded tails, under the furnace of flames; all of the porcelain, painted gargoyles, trembled and cracked in terror on their cavern perches.

Then all the hundreds, of little, warning rubescent bells of the pagoda, quivered and quavered, with the heated desire to ring out the danger.

All the green and gold tiles of the temple were melting, the wooden goldfish above them, were writhing vermillion, against the sky.

The flaming, ebony demon, flew high above the heads of the palace guards, through the blue, black, fog of smoke, mingled with incense.

Song Li heard the cacophony of calamity, emanating from the heavenly heights' temple, she calmed her mind, and shook her spirit awake.

We must save the great palace, of the mother goddess, her mind cried to her inner self.

Surely, we must! Then she made a magical sign, recited a special spell, clenched her claws tightly, shook her body, and jumped up, launching herself into the skies, as she sprayed pheromones to her hive-mind.

She commanded her bees to collect water, from the rainmaker clouds congregated on the horizon. Out of the blue, hundreds, then thousands, then millions of honeybees came soaring, each carrying in their pollen buckets of water. As the squadron of apian came to the terrible conflagration, every worker dropped their drops of water, down, down, down it fell, until it made a column of white rainbows rising into the heavens.

Finally, the fomenting fury had been doused, and the imperial palace redeemed.

A time of famine came to the Flamboyant flower mountains, scout, and forager bees were sailing out every day, forever scanning the distant horizons for their hives sustenance.

Soaring from grass, to tree, to bush, searching for nectar, pollen and propolis, but as far as they flew, the flowers seemed too far, and too few.

The bees of the golden promise hive clambered over, and under each other, to rally to their designations, and the seething mass of apian pressed at the very walls of their congested home.

The whole width of the entrance was engorged with foraging workers. Inside the waxen walls, temperatures and tempers were heated.

Displeased with this disharmony, Supreme ruler, Lieu Hanh called to her disciple, Song Li: "Overpopulation is natures imbalance, and this cannot stand. It is time for change, a division of the great, golden promise hive.

It is time to have a 'supersedure!'

Song Li, you will take three quarters of the hive to a new location, and make a prestigious, revived hive, with your faithful workers."

The Queen called her best scout bees together, giving them this dictum:

"As you travel, you are to examine the way carefully. Do not journey high in the air, but remain at an altitude, halfway between haze and cloud, so you can see the mountains and waters, and remember the exact distance to the locality, where nectar filled blooms are most prolific".

Scout bees took off to the north, the south, the west, and the east; in every corner of the realm the small searchers scoured.

They used all their facilities, to perceive the journey of their expedition, for they all knew that the hive was getting overwrought.

Queen Song Li's pheromonal essence was becoming diffused, Lieu Hanh would not conscious an instability of this nature!

At last, they found themselves flying beneath the shadows of blossoms, along a path covered in moss, and using their antenna, they detected the delicate, magnetic ambrosia, of mangrove forests, and they drove in that direction.

Li Lou, the far-seeing explorer, was the golden promise hive's most experienced scout, she could even see a dragonfly, spread its wings at a thousand feet.

From her lofty height, Li Lou espied strange flowers, rivalling the sun in brightness, crape myrtle trees, matching well, the clear sky in blueness, the finest floral sight in the east. The streams spilt chips of jade, pomegranates, with brocade-like pouches, and a curvate band of bamboos, like clouds outstretched.

Truly, it could be called a Shangri la on Earth, and Li Lou could not take her eyes off this wondrous place.

Magically, in daylight, scout Li Lou, could discern good from evil, she knew that new accommodation had to bee protected from the elements, it had to have a small entrance, at the bottom of a cavity, it must have warmth from the sun, and not be infested with ants.

Li Lou had seen a giant, spiraling, strangler fig tree, with many hive sites, at the very centre of a clearing, near the tinkling, chicken-bone, jade waterfalls!

"This will bee the new palace of brightness", she piped to the other guide scouts.

The bees shook, with excited buzzing, all speaking at once, they had to have eighty percent agreement to the location.

If less agreement, the main workers, and Queen Song Li, would have no confidence in their choice.

In early summer, time ran forward to the day the swarm had to depart, the convergence of lives into new hives.

The impermanence of natural life, that Song Li had meditated on, in her long convalescence in the amber prism, deep within the heartbroken mountain, was upon her.

The colony had been quiet as the nursery bees worked, constructing queen cups to feed the new princess bees, who would take the Queens place in the original nest.

The hundreds of intrepid voyager bees, had gorged themselves on honey, holding reserves in their honey crops for their journey, to a new hive home.

New Queen eggs were laid, and Song Li lost half her body weight for the expedition so she could fly, and only her faithful attendant, Cinderbee, fed her royal jelly.

The whole migration must only take up to three days before their nectar stores ran out!

The hive began its ascension; ten thousand bees were to become one thousand. Throngs of worker bees transmuted, into multitudinous beams of blazing luminosity, a tail star, chasing the scout bees!

As they departed, four formidable new queens hatched, and the cycle of supremacy began anew.

Song Li's lightweight body flew like thistle down with the absconding swarms. Suddenly, out of the diamanté sky, richly coloured plumage caught the Queens eyes.

A blue bearded bee-eater launched itself directly at her; urgently, Song Li veered, this way and that, but finally, the avian had her in its clutches.

Out of the blue came Cinderbee, flying as fast and as furiously as she could, rallying to save her Queen, Song Li, from the bird's long, curved beak, but alas, her soaring aerobatics, and life-ending sting, could not dissuade the bee-eater from grasping onto its prey even tighter.

The bird flapped its turquoise wings, springing away from the swarm, and a decimated Cinderbee, fell amongst her compatriots; they caught the brave little bee as she swooned.

Her only sting, sacrificed for her majestic monarch, Cinderbee's broken body, was gently carried away by her companions, to the new nest, in the palace of brightness, and there, she became a part of the legacy of Song Li, Queen Mother of the grand promise hive.

Song Li looked up at her predator, she heard the call of nature, she saw its beaded, bejewels eyes winking in the sunlight, and then she saw no more.

Sparks of light, shone through a mosaic of mists, the silver stream aglow, the air was perfectly pure, the sky, full of bright twinkling stars.

All sounds were hushed, until the buzz of courageous Cinderbee, and daring drone Tan Viet, filled the emptiness.

Song Li's eyes were opened, and there before her, stood Lieu Hanh, Grand Goddess of the worlds below, and above. "Song Li she said, devoted disciple, you have been tested, and you have triumphed over all your adversaries.

You will forever fly amongst celestial, apricot blossoms, and be immortalised for your obedience to Mother Nature's lores, all will know of you, and bee glad!"

Glossary

Abdomen: soft posterior of bee with a striped appearance used for –

- Defence - sheathes the stinger and venom sac
- Digestion - contains honey stomach for nectar storage, processes food and excretes waste.
- Glands - Encases the wax making gland and a scent gland
- Navigating - honeybees have magnetic qualities that use the earth and sun as a compass
- Reproduction - the abdomen houses the reproductive organs of the drones and the queen.

Antennae - bee antennae are moveable and wave around, they distinguish vibrations, fragrances, even electrical fields and movement. They identify and discriminate multi-sensory clues from blossoms, using touch, sight, smell, taste.

Apis - Latin for Bee

Apis Cerana - Eastern honeybee, an Asiatic native to Southern, Southeast and Eastern Asia, Afghanistan, Australia, Bhutan, China, Indonesia, India, Japan, North Korea, South Korea, Laos, Malaysia, Mongolia, Nepal, New Guinea, Pakistan, Philippines, Taiwan, Thailand, Tibet, Vietnam.

Builds nests comprising of numerous combs in cavities, with tiny entrances. They survive on a diet of pollen, nectar, and honey.

Apis Melefora - honey-bearing. Called a western honeybee, originating in Africa then spread to the Middle East and Europe, they are now found on every continent except Antarctica. These honeybees were the first domesticated insects and beekeepers still keep these bees for their honey production today.

Beeline - the belief that a bee, when it is finished collecting pollen will take the briefest passage back to its hive without delay or meandering. A direct course but also denotes that there is some urgency behind the activity.

Bee-bread - also called bee pollen or ambrosia, a ball of field gathered flower pollen packed by worker honeybees as a primary food for the hive.

Bee-brood - means honeybee eggs, larvae and pupae at various stages of development in the honeycombs.

Bee-catcher bird - groups of small birds with richly coloured plumage, slender bodies, long tail feathers, and curved long bills. These avians eat insects, bees and wasps caught whilst flying.

Buffalo dung - Asian honeybees collect animal dung and apply spots of it around the entry to hives to deter the deadly nest raids by Vespa soror wasps/hornets.

Cocoon - a protective casing spun by bees; cocoon spinning occurs when the bee transitions from larvae to pupa.

Compound eyes- bees have five eyes, two compound eyes on the sides of their heads and three ocelli eyes on the top of their heads. Compound eyes help bee perceive objects from different angles. Oceilli eyes see colour, shapes and sizes. Bee eyes are hairy and sense changes in the wind for flight.

Cone of drone- traffic cone shape, drone bees make when chasing the queen bee in the nuptial flight.

Dragon ghost mantis- A Vietnamese rare praying mantis resembling a leaf, possessing a camouflaged appearance, perfect for hunting insects. It lives in humid rainforest areas in Asia.

The fire was added for imaginary allegory in this story.

Drone congregation area - intergenerational meeting place for drones from different hives hovering thirty feet in the air. Their large compound eyes see and identify the queen in mid-air.

Exoskeleton - bee / insect body covering, armour or skeletal system made of tough resilient chitin.

The moulting of this body covering cuticle is called exuviae.

Fanning bees - when the hive is in danger of overheating the water carrying bees obtain cooling water and bring it back to spread on the backs of fanning worker bees.

Ventilation of the hive eventually expels both excess water and heat into the outside world.

Fireback pheasants- these fabulous, colourful birds, inhabit evergreen tropical forests in lowlands and hills, they hide in patches of bamboo and palms. The male is iridescent blue black with a white crest , red legs and red facial skin. The female is a coppery brown, very few of these birds survive now in the wild.

Heat balling - A defence mechanism used by honeybees. When an invader threatens the hive, the honeybees get into an all-encompassing ball around their prey, the bees then heat up their thoraxes by exercising their flight muscles to above 45 degrees, which is lethal for predator victim!

Hexagon - six-sided figure, the perfect geometric shape for storing honey in a hive.

Hive/nest - the honeybee colony's home, housing made in a natural cavity, rock or wood. The internal structure is made up of a densely packed group of hexagonal prismatic cells made of beeswax called honeycomb. Used to store food (honey, nectar, pollen) and house bee brood (eggs, larvae, pupae)

Honey - honeybees produce honey by amassing and distilling flower nectar. Bees value honey for its sugars and energy to fly with.

Bees stockpile honey for themselves, lean times and wintering.

When nectar is abundant it can take a forager bee more than an hour of unflagging work to gather enough honey to fill its honey crop.

Arriving back at the hive the foragers regurgitate and convey nectar to hive workers. Once it is in their stomachs hive bees regurgitate the honey continuously forming a bubble between their mandibles (pair of jaws) speeding its digestion and concentration.

Hornet - Vespa Mandarina -; Japanese hornet or wasp, body length 1 3/4 inches

Wingspan 3 inches / stinger 1/4 inch injects powerful venom. Primarily a forest dweller and low mountain foothills. Lives in subterranean nests in rotted pine roots. This predator can fly 100 kilometres in one day, it is five times the size of a honeybee and heavily armoured. A single Vespa can kill forty bees per minute and several hornets can wipe out a whole colony of Apis cerana or Apis melaflora. It kills quickly, decapitating its victim with huge mandibles, drinks its juices then chews the insects body into a paste to feed its larvae. Being stung by this hornet is like having a burning spike driven into your body.

Imago - The final adult stage of an insect, mature with wings

King cobra snake- an ophidian, one of the world's longest poisonous snakes, found in India, Southeast Asia and Southern China. After envenomation, it eats other snakes, lizards and small rodents whole. It is an elapid (has a neck flap that it spreads when alarmed, rising its head showing its fangs. hissing and charging) only when it is threatened. These ophidians are coloured olive green to black with white strips to unbroken umber-brown grey. They have big eyes with amber irises and round pupils.

They shed their skin 4 to 6 times a year this is called ecolysis, rubbing themselves against rough surfaces and wriggling a lot.

Moulting - shedding the exoskeleton, there are five moults of the honeybee larvae to go through before pupae stage and adulthood.

Nuptial flight- circular flight as the queen emits pheromones/ scent attracting drones from up to 1 kilometre away. The queen collects and stores seeds of drone bees in her body for the rest of her life.

Pollen - pollen grains from flowering plant anthers stick to the honeybee's hairy bodies, this helps with pollination from flower to flower, the collected pollen is scrapped off by the worker bees and made into a ball or pellet, then packed by the bees as a primary source of food for the hive it is called bee bread or ambrosia.

Pollen packing - A tarsal on the back leg brushes off the pollen, which is made into bee bread.

Propolis - Also known as bee glue - made up of resin collected from plants and transformed by mixing bee saliva, beeswax and resin.

*Used for thermal insulation

*Reinforcement of the structure of the hive

*Protection from pathogens

Royal jelly - milky substance worker bee secretes from the top of their heads. Made of proteins, simple sugars, fatty acids and vitamins with antibacterial and antibiotic components. Queen bee sticks her tongue out to be fed by the workers, she never feeds herself, she is a queen!

Stages of worker bees

Cleaner bees (0 to 3 days) Cleanses the hive for the first 3 days after emergence, eliminates dead larvae and debris from the nest.

Wax Bees female bees (5 to 9 days old) Once wax gland located on underside of abdomen is operational. Starts making combs, reuses old wax to reinforce cracks and crevices in hive walls and entrance.

Nurse Bees (3 to 14 days old). Younger female bees feeding and caring for eggs, larvae, pupae, queen, drones consuming pollen and activating the hypo- pharyngeal gland in their head to produce royal jelly.

Guard & sentry Bees (18 to 21 days old) Female bees who protect hive from intruders/predators.

Scout Bees (21 to 35 days old) Accomplished foragers who locate best flowers for nectar/ pollen. Also pinpoint new hive sites, there are only 500 scout bees in every 10,000 bees.

Drones - male Bees (24 days to mature from egg/larvae/pupae to hatching adult)

Has a lifespan of around 60 days, this male bee has no stinger and does not gather nectar or pollen. They are fed by the female worker bees and are the only male bees in the colony. Their main purpose in the hive is to fly out to a congregation waiting area (natural gathering site for honey bees to mate) and wait for a queen from a different hive to fly by. They attempt to mate with this queen, forty metres above the ground, these bees die rapidly after mating.

Drones have large eyes to distinguish the queen as she flies through hundreds of other drones, as well as antenna to smell a queen as an identifiable signal.

Queen Bee (16 days egg/larvae/pupae/adult.) Lays up to 2,000 eggs per day, the only bee to produce workers for hive. Can live up to seven years; she only leaves the colony to mate with drones and when the hive swarms. Uses pheromones/scent to signal her commands to her worker bees

Stomachs - Bees have two stomach compartments -

One for storing nectar and transportation (called the honey crop)

One for digesting food and nutrients

*Bees can carry half their body weight in nectar (50 mg)

Supersedure - the bee colony desires to expand and establish a new hive, usually in early summer - This is initiated by the construction of new queen cells, the old hive will lose 3/4 of its bees, in the move.

Swarming - Process of a single colony splitting into two or more different colonies.

A large swarm of bees leaves the original hive and rests in a cluster on a nearby tree branch. Waiting for scout bees to relay the new hive location (usually within a few hours). Usually in springtime or early summer.

Waggle dance - a figure eight series of movements scouting bees make on return to hive yielding nectar, water sources housing locations information.

Accommodates the changing direction of the sun

Run in straight line waggling torso side to side in direct of food

Turn and circle back to starting point

Alternate direction left to right.

Repeat many times

Direction of waggle run relative to hive indicates direction of hive

Length of waggle dance indicates the distance

Wax moth - lays eggs in the crevices of honeycombs, larvae feed on the mid rib of the combs, the honey leaks out and the bee offspring die. The wax moth larvae tunnel through combs, spinning silk linings that entangle bee lava, the emerging bees starve and die.

Winter cluster - The bees cling tightly together on the combs of the hive. The temperature inside the hive remains warm, bees survive winter cold.

www.ingramcontent.com/pod-product-compliance
Lightning Source LLC
Chambersburg PA
CBRC092340290426
44109CB00008B/167